GODMAKER
±

Godmaker

ALR007

Published by

Aqualamb

Godmaker is:
Pete Ross : Vocals / Guitar
Andrew Archey : Bass
Jon Lane : Drums
Chris Strait : Guitar / Vocals

Drums recorded in August 2013 at The Audio Parlour by Justin Mantooth

Guitars, Bass, Vocals recorded November 2013 at Continental Recording Studio by Phil Duke

Mixed at West End Studios by Justin Mantooth

Mastered at Eureka Mastering by Mike Nolte

Designed by Eric Palmerlee

Image Credits
Joe Silver: Cover art and pgs 52-53
Stephen Wilson: Title page illustrations and lettering. Photos on pgs 15, 16-17, 38-39, 59, 60-61, 66-67, 80, 88
Rob Menzer: Photos on pgs 20-21, 40-41, 42-43, 44, 46-47, 68-69, 70-71, 72-73, 74-75, 90-91, 92-93
Tracey Noelle Luz: Photos on pgs 18-19, 22-23, 98. Phil Duke: Photo on pgs 54-55
Steve "DRS" Martinez: Photos on pgs 48-49. Dan "Irish" Merritt: pgs 94-95
Brian Froustet: Photo on pgs 24-25. Steve Voegele: Photo on pg 45

10 9 8 7 6 5 4 3 2 1 First Printing
ISBN: 978-0692308240

aqualamb.org / godmakerbk.com

CONTENTS

The music for this release can be downloaded
via the link below:

http://aqualamb.org/007

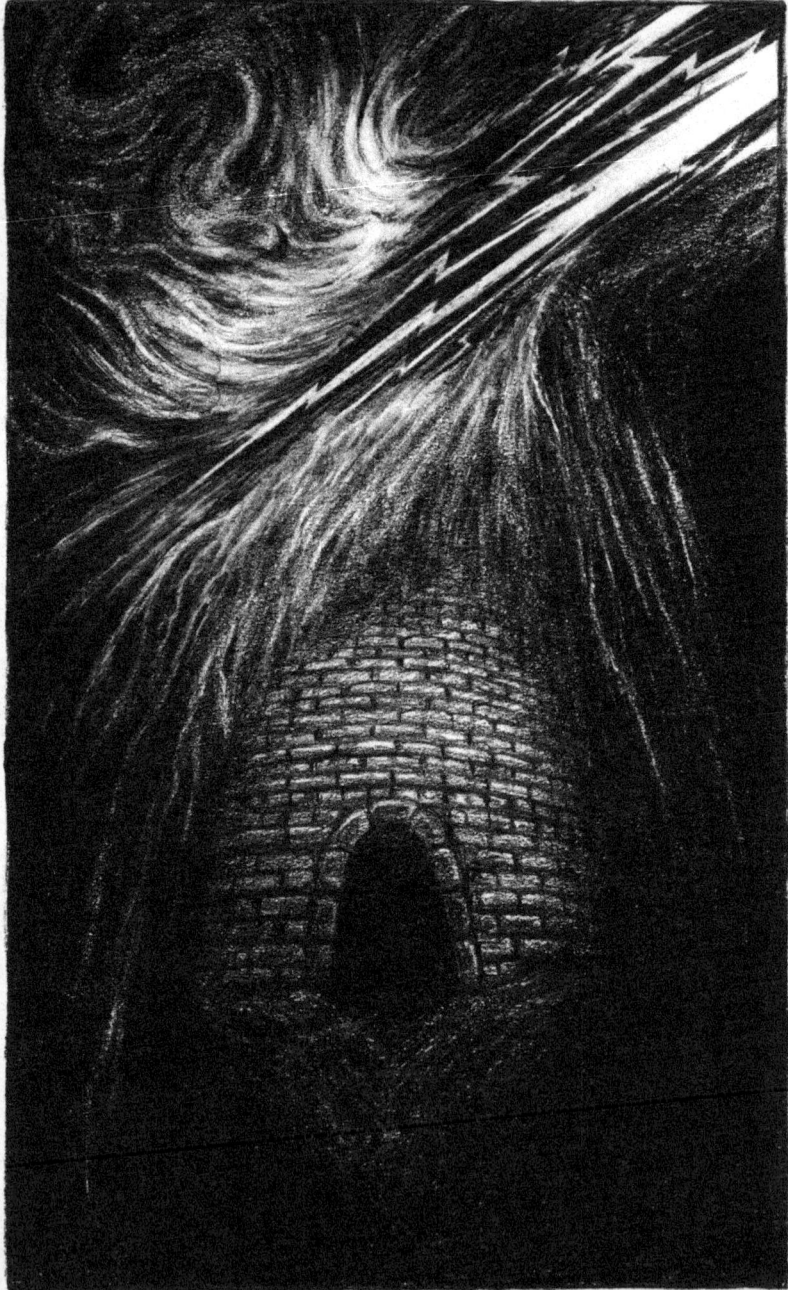

I

MEGALITH

GIVE
TAKE
LIVE
WAKE

when I was a little boy
daddy stole all of my toys

before the stars...
before the trees...

before the stars - eyes of the dead
before the trees - disease our bread
before the storm - filling my head
before ocean - (ice and) septic days of draining hope

but in stages - it is revealed

soul is deceived - terrestrial
feed me the need - material
knowing I bleed - eventual
be done with me - your ritual

but in stages - I will be reborn

my inner child slept
years unaware but not alone
universe in reflection
in eyes of man is known

but in stages - it is revealed
to no other man or prophet
do I kneel

DO I KNEEL???

I will be reborn

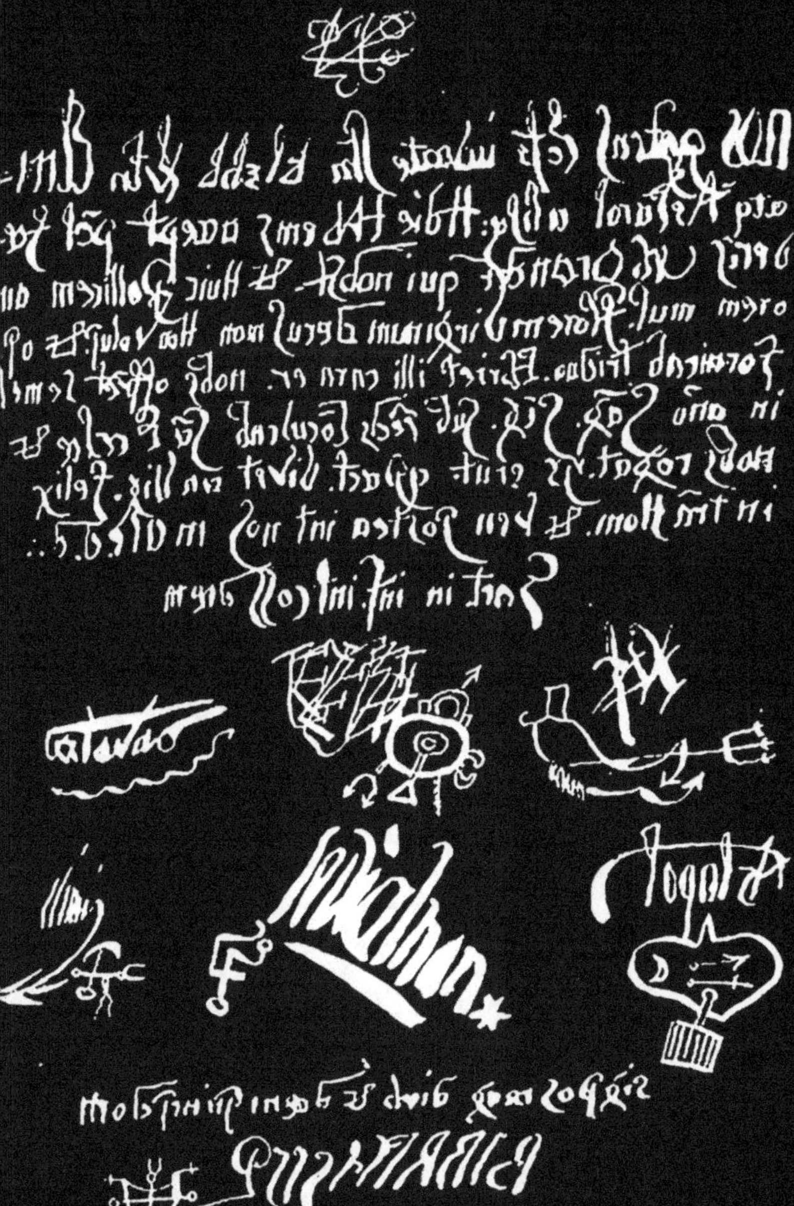

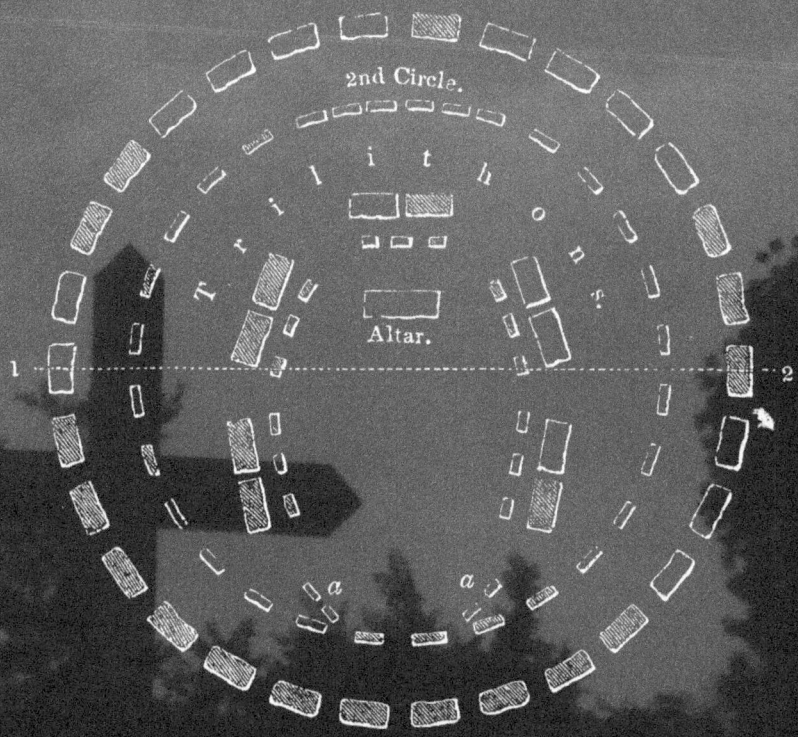

2nd Circle.

Trilithons.

Altar.

1 - 2

a   a

ALPHA DRACONIS

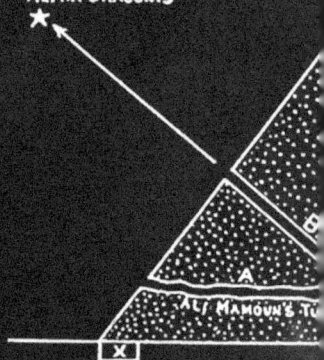

★

A

B

ALI MAMOUN'S T

X

CAPSTONE

N

V.V.   V.V.

G

R

M
T P
Q
C
K

GRAND GALLERY

J   Q

PASSAGE

W

S

SCENDING PASSAGE

B

H

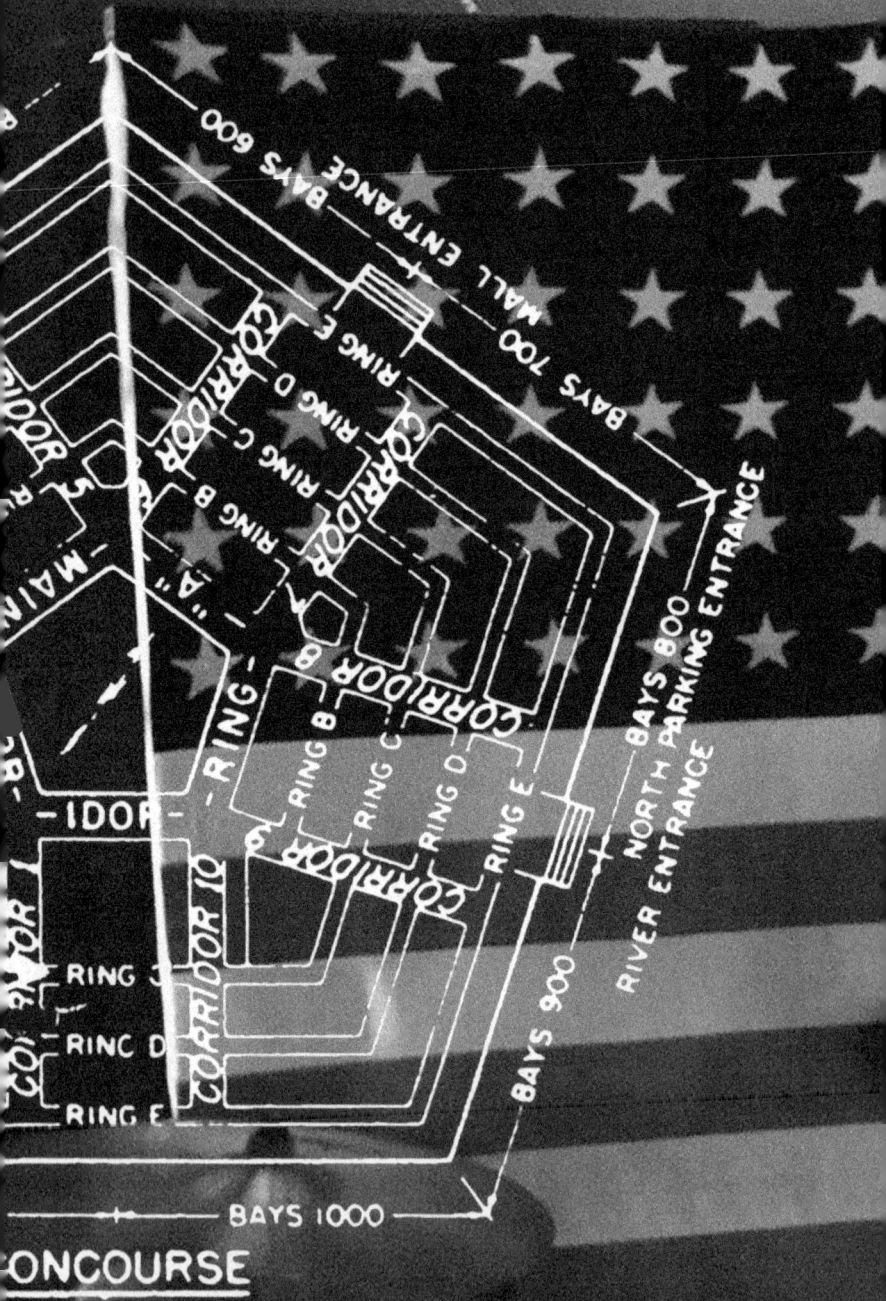

BAYS 600

MALL ENTRANCE

BAYS 700

NORTH PARKING ENTRANCE

BAYS 800

RIVER ENTRANCE

BAYS 900

BAYS 1000

CONCOURSE

RING E

RING D

RING C

RING B

"A"

CORRIDOR

CORRIDOR 5

MAIN

CORRIDOR

RING A

RING B

RING C

RING D

RING E

CORRIDOR 10

CORRIDOR

-IDOR-

RING J

RING D

RING E

COR

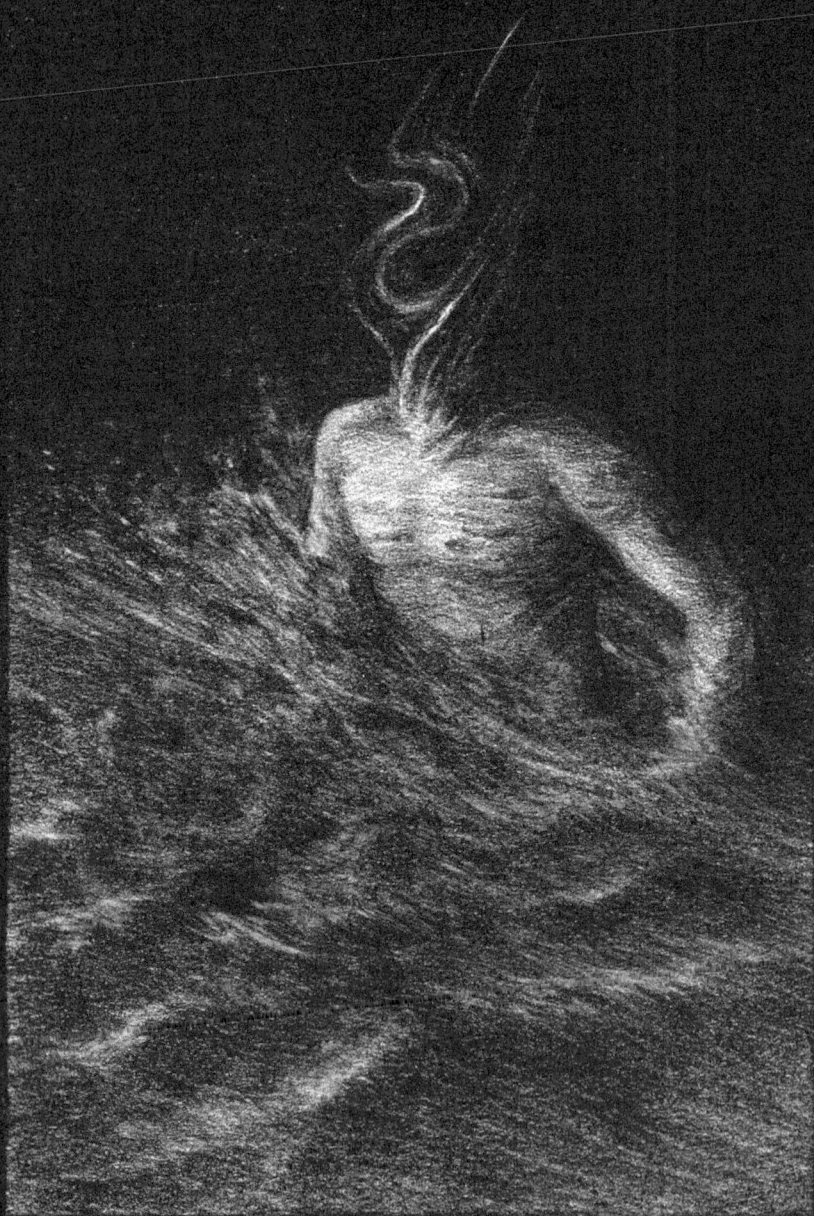

II

SHALLOW
POINTS

RISE

love, suffer and live without a smile - hope it binds,
hope it burns, hope it kills.
cross shards of any hope at all.
hope is done.
...and the water opens wide...

keep it away
down in the drain
now in our grave
robbed of our way

...and the water opens wide...
...and the water opens –

washes the ground from under me
years of crashing waves have worn me razor sharp,
razor thin... razors in, and the water opens wide...

racing on to shallow points
wading on to shallow points
holding on to shallow points
wading on from shallow points

one more step away from land
all that's left that was a man
rusts away all of my plans
swallows everything I am

DROWN

...and the water opens...

NORTH HORIZON

Algenib

Capella

AURIGA

CASSIOP

CAMELOPARDALIS

CEPH

POLE
STAR

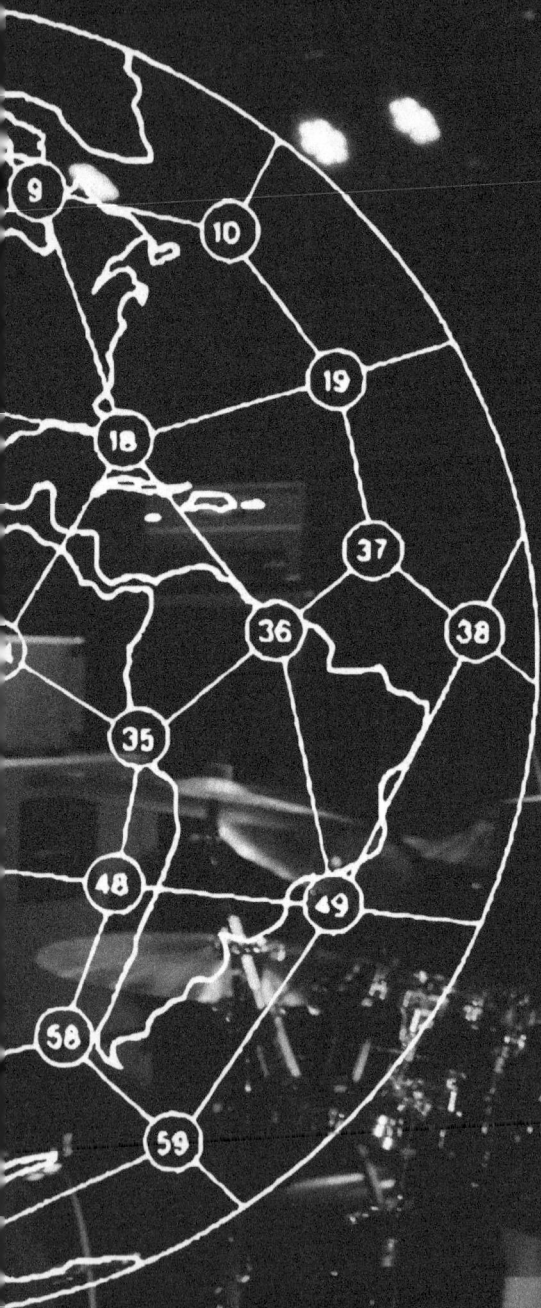

III

DESK MURDER

wading through the bile and piss
clinging on with empty fists
a voice inside my head says "scream!"

one day I will get through this
'til then, I'll just live with it
I will not let this confine me
I want to be me

now it's time to go
hurry it up - just go
now it's time to go
now is the time

hands in pockets to persist
however long this must exist
a voice inside my head still screams

one day I will get through this
'til then, I'll just deal with it
I'll never let this define me
I want to be me

now it's time to pay

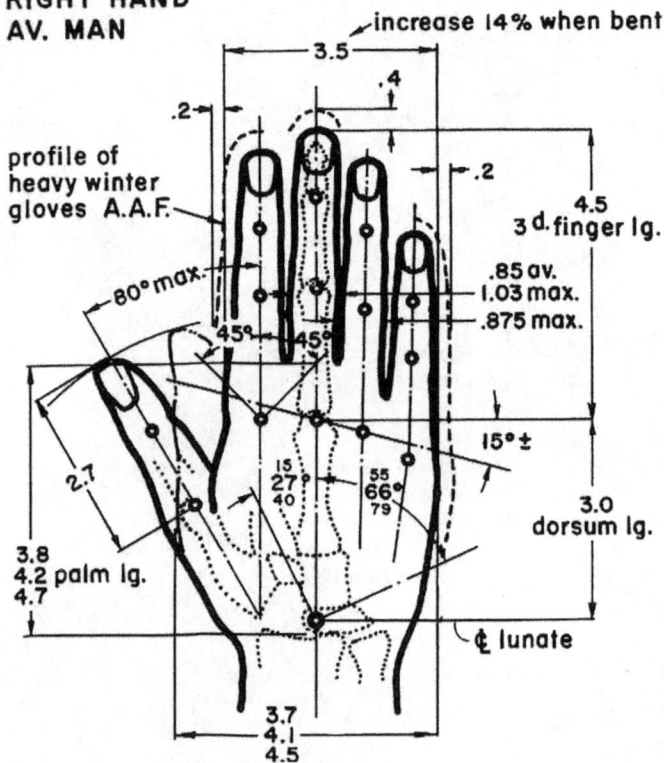

RIGHT HAND
AV. MAN

increase 14% when bent

3.5

.4

.2

profile of
heavy winter
gloves A.A.F.

.2

4.5
3 d. finger lg.

80° max.

.85 av.
1.03 max.
.875 max.

45° 45°

15° ±

15
27°
40

55
66°
79

3.0
dorsum lg.

2.7

₵ lunate

3.8
4.2 palm lg.
4.7

3.7
4.1
4.5

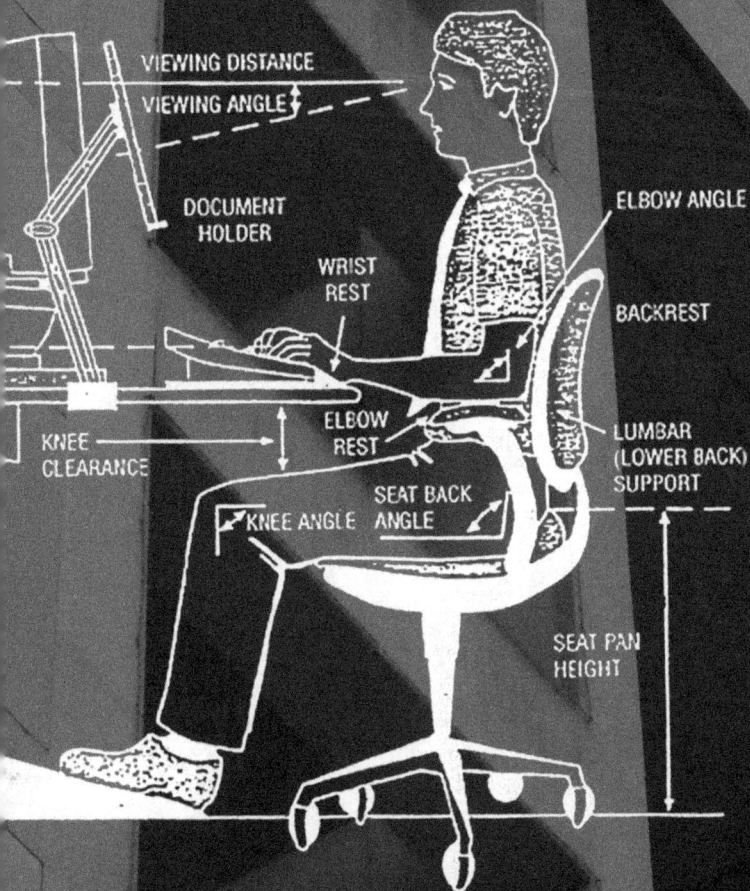

VIEWING DISTANCE

VIEWING ANGLE

DOCUMENT HOLDER

WRIST REST

ELBOW ANGLE

BACKREST

LUMBAR (LOWER BACK) SUPPORT

KNEE CLEARANCE

ELBOW REST

KNEE ANGLE

SEAT BACK ANGLE

SEAT PAN HEIGHT

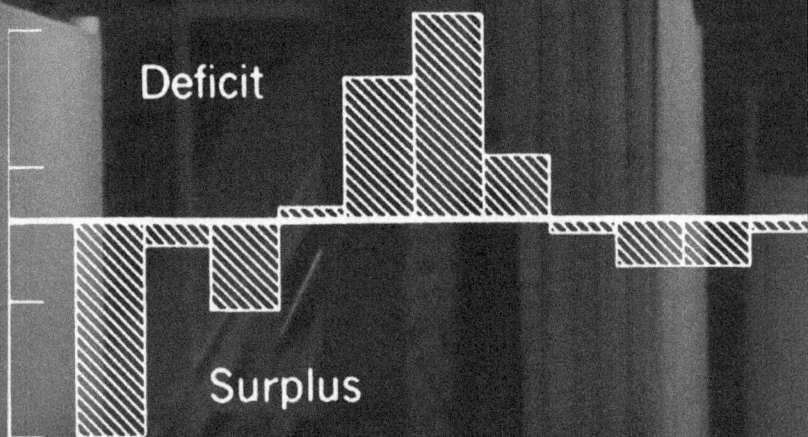

Deficit

Surplus

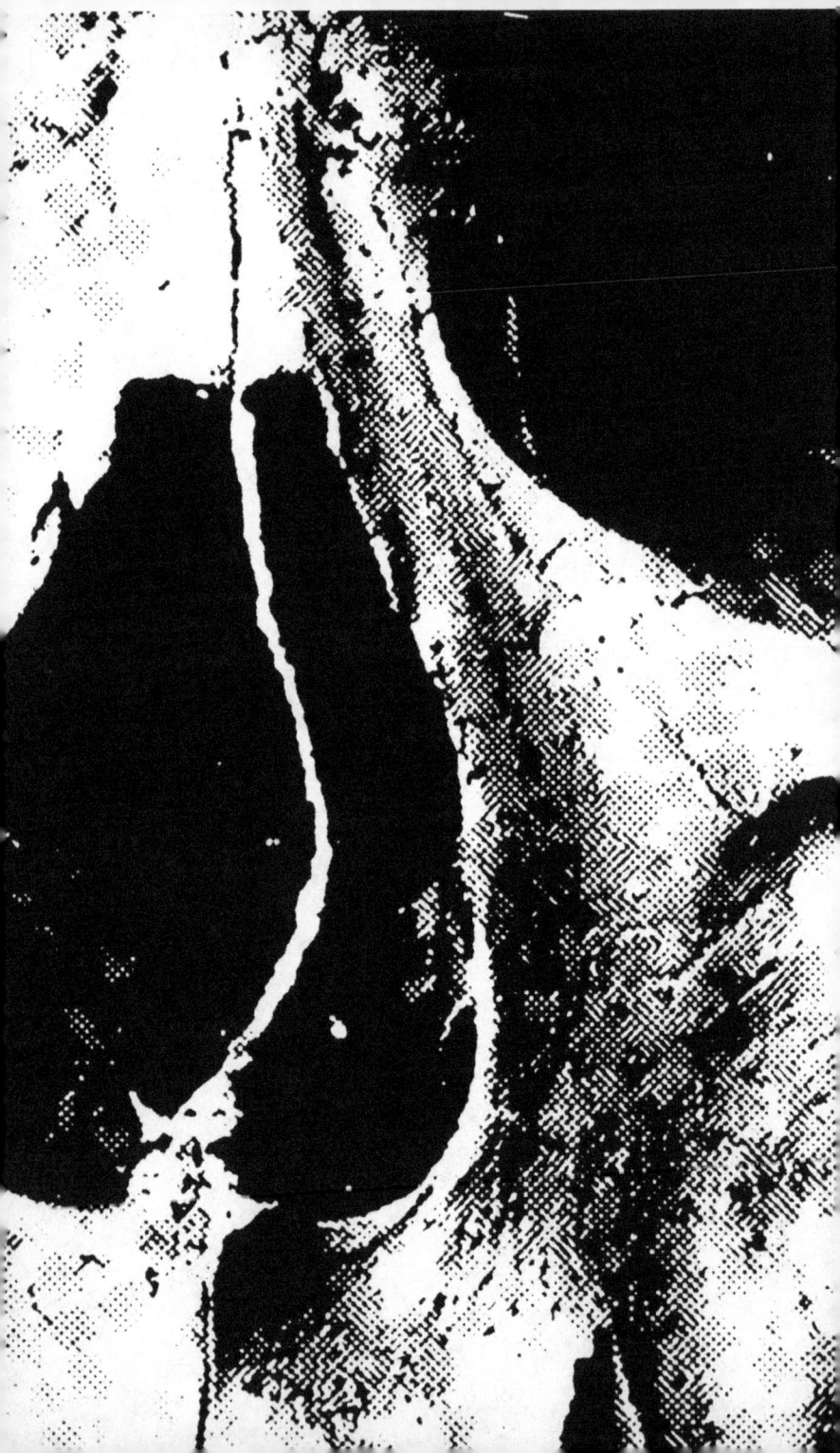

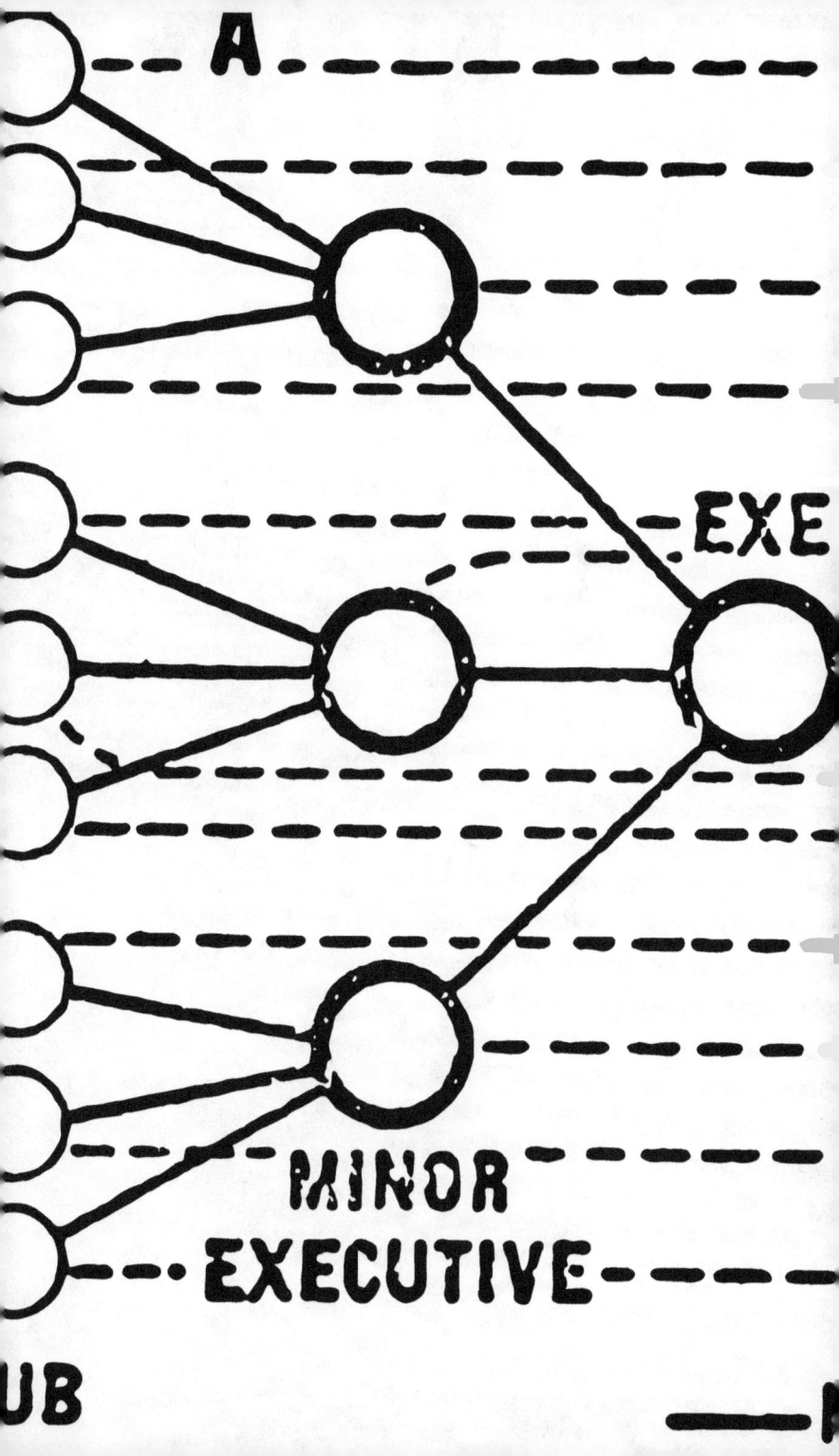

IV

FADED GLORY

goin' in at the ceiling
goin' in – adrift a specimen
goin' in at the ceiling
goin' in – at the center of space I am

sever ties

shut me out
shut me in
sever ties, sever from within
shut me in
shut me out
welcome to the science of shutting down

sever everything

you've got so much to say
watch me walking away
you've got so much to say

goin' in at the ceiling
goin' in....

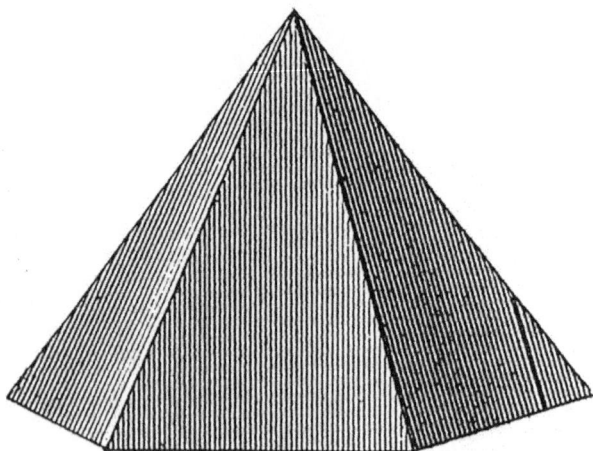

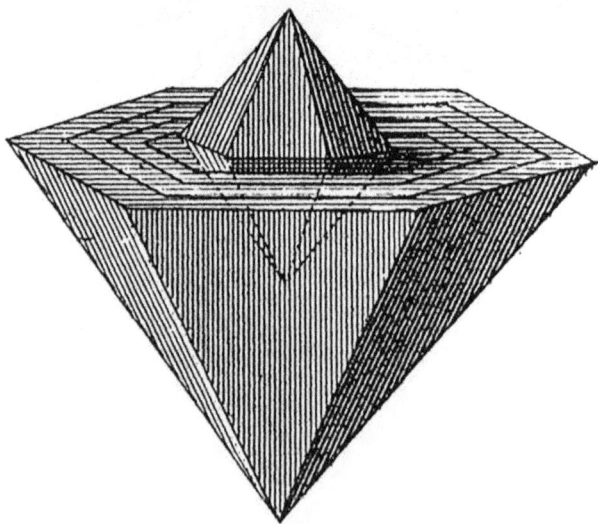

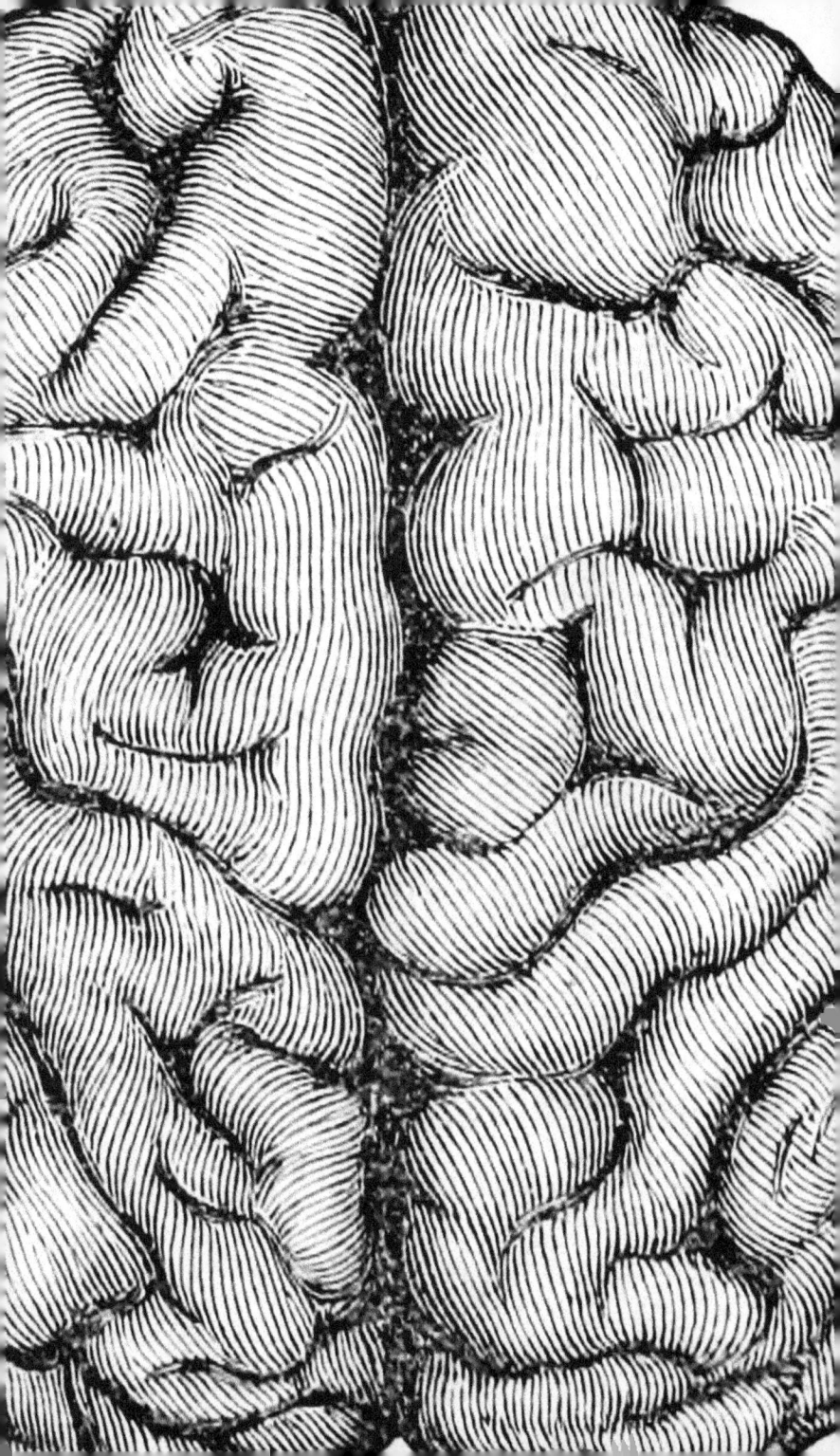

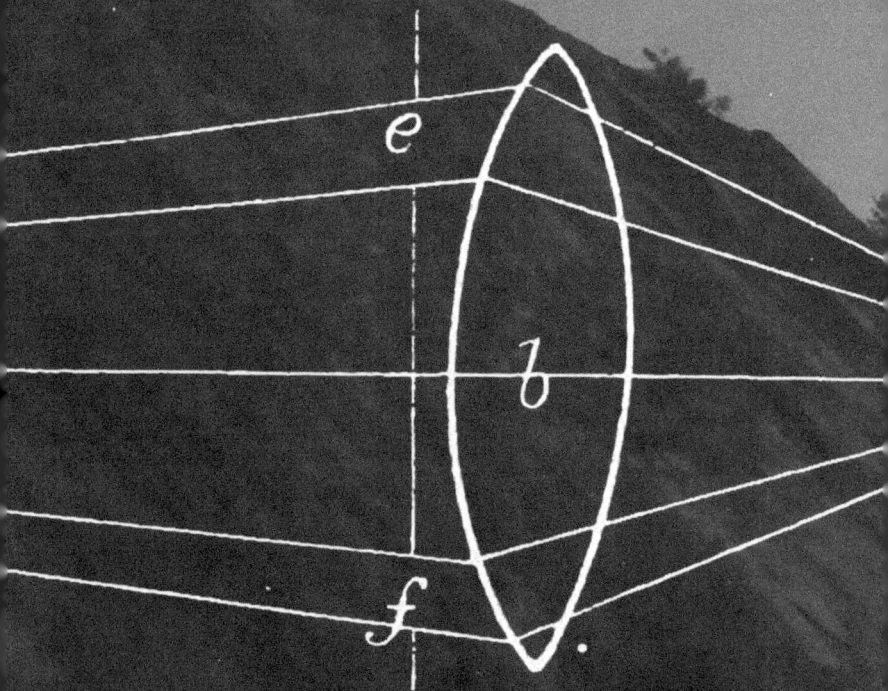

e

b

f

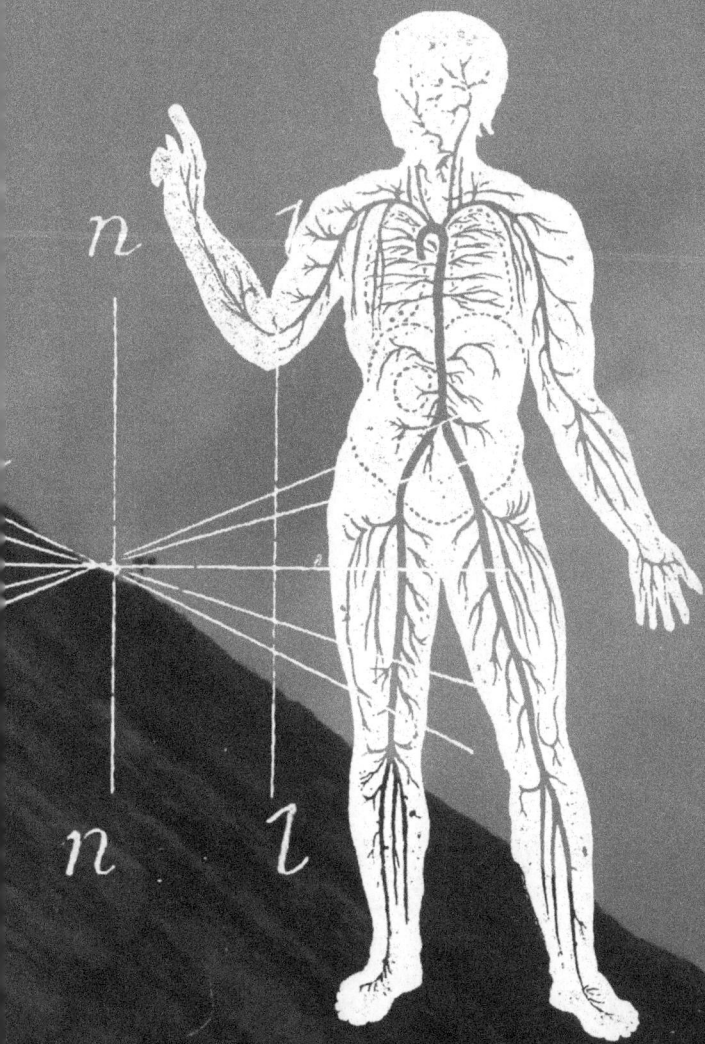

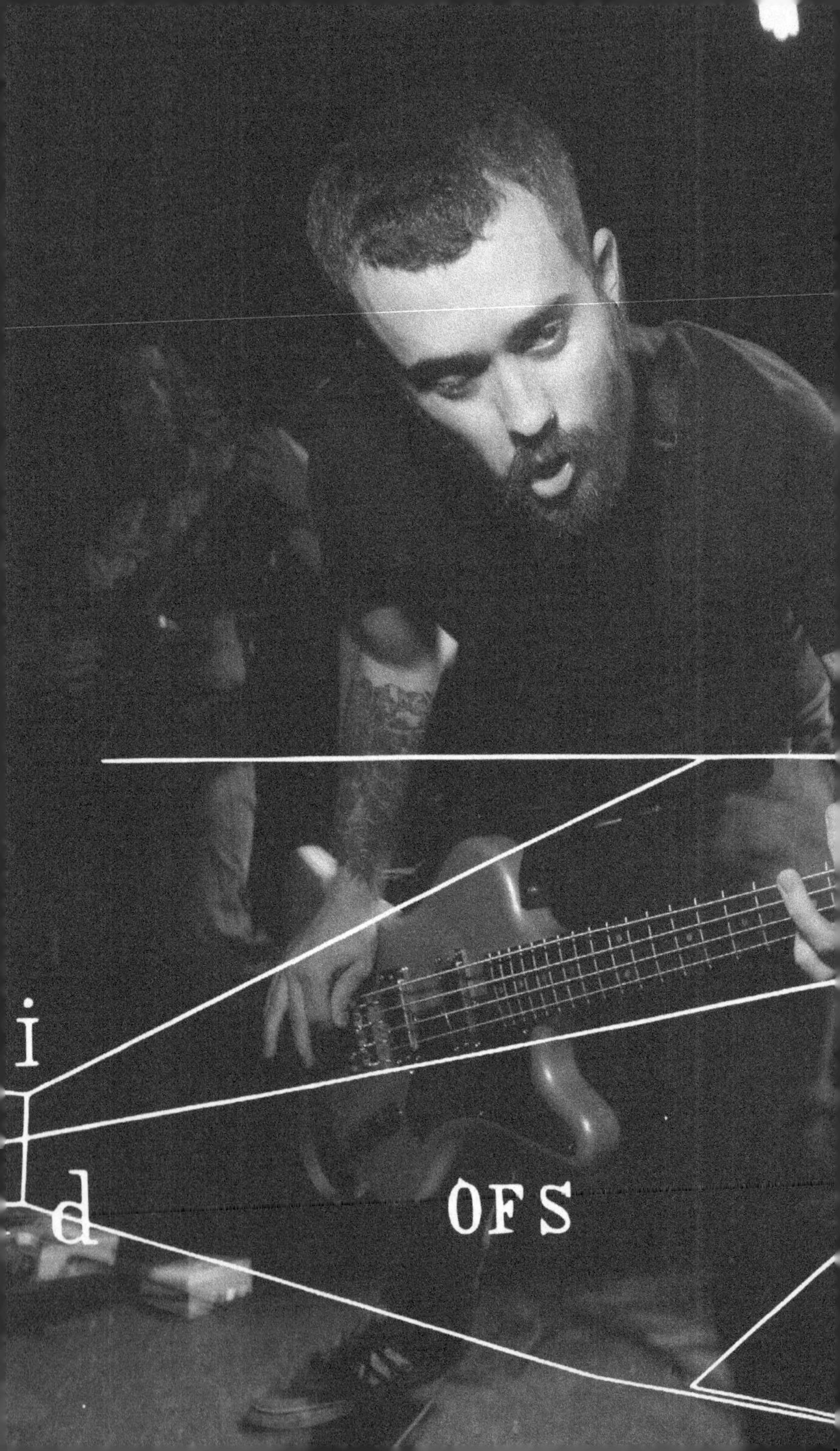
i
d
OFS

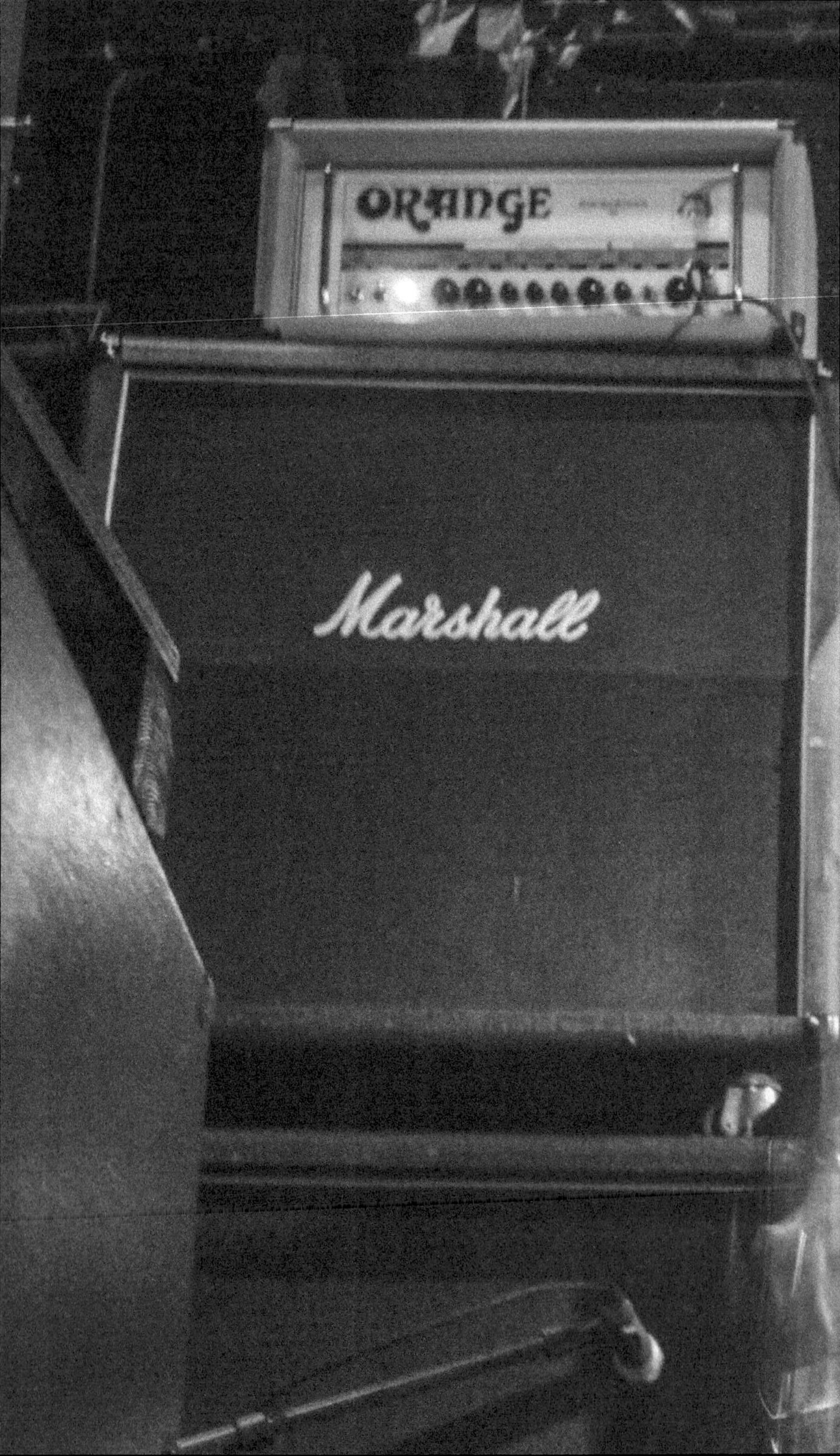
ORANGE
Marshall

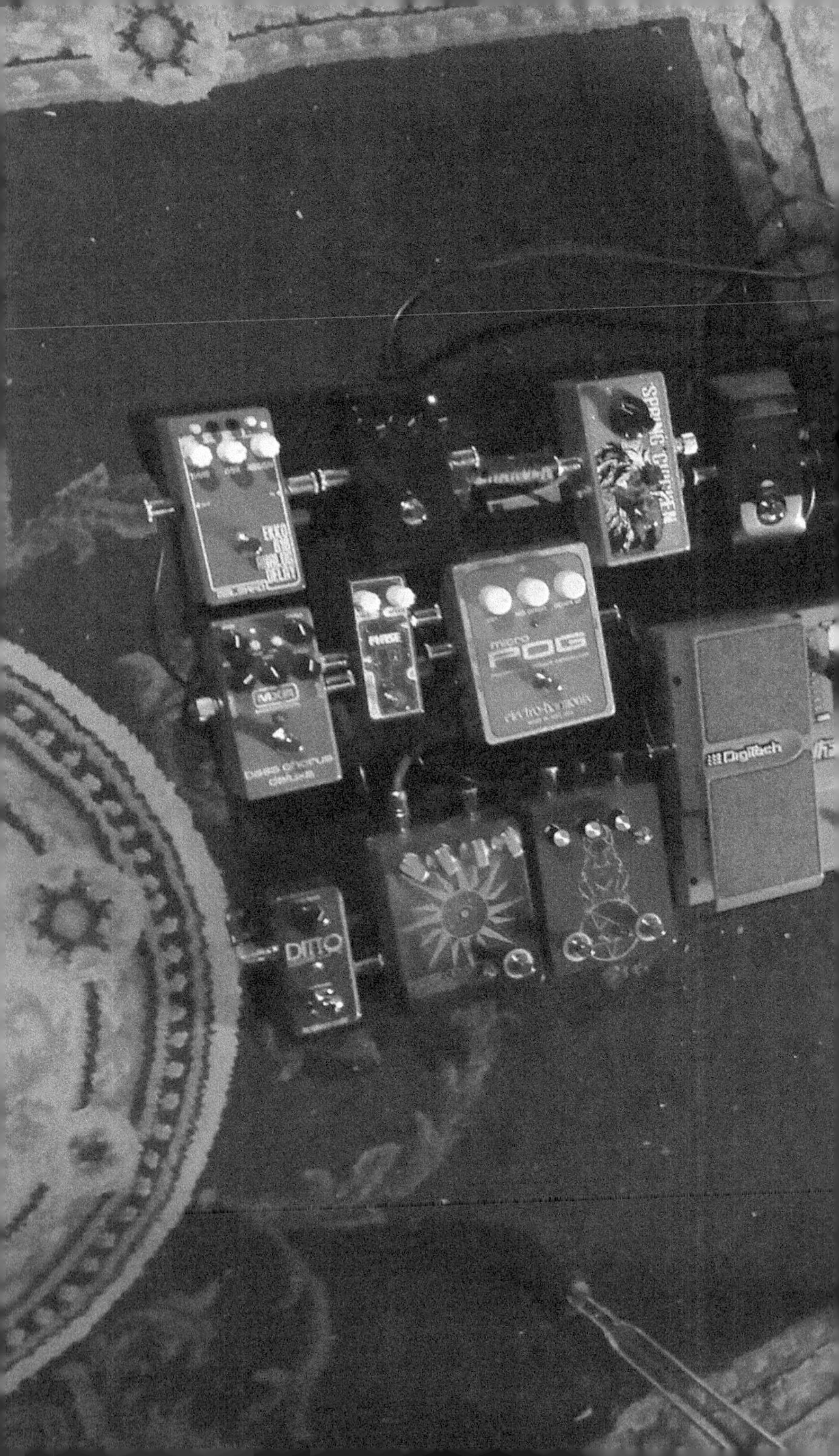
DigiTech
micro POG
MXR
DITTO

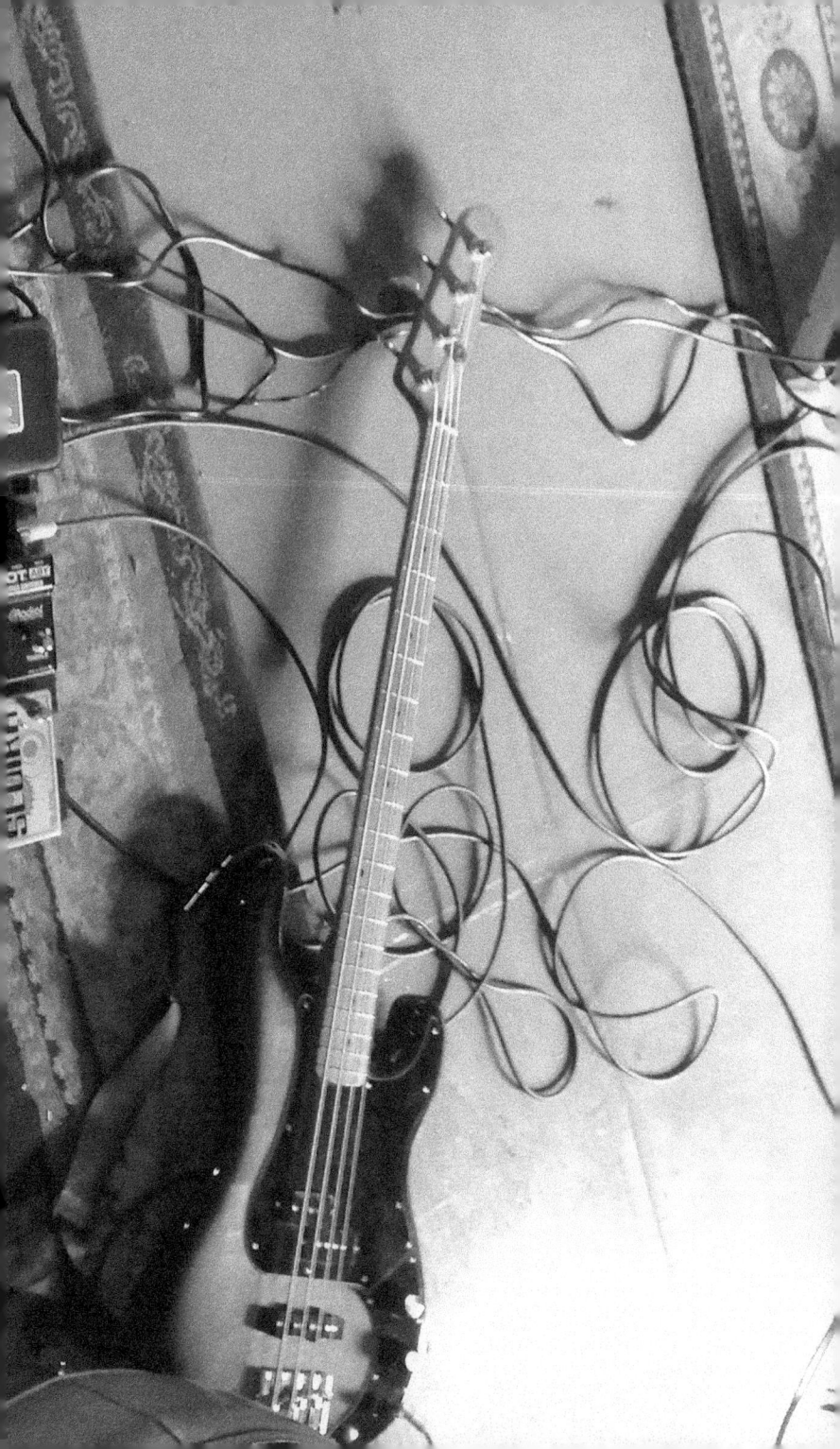

SATAN LOVES YOU

THANK YOU

Jimmy Archey
Joe Silver
Jeff St. Filmer
Stephen Wilson
Jess "Mama Godmaker" Coppinger
Frank Huang
Bryan "Godbaker" Gittleman
Dave Castillo
Arty Shepherd
George Souleidis
Ryan & Shannon Ratajski
Justin Mantooth
Phil Duke
Mike Nolte
Our Sweet Buchina (RIP)
Drew Mack
Nick Cageao
Jay Morris
Danny Katz
Luis Hernandez
Eric Palmerlee
Johnathan Swafford
Steve Gordon
Tracey Noelle Luz
Steve "DRS" Martinez
Dan "Irish" Merritt
Rob Menzer
Brian Froustet
Steve Voegele
Rozamov
Cleanteeth
White Widows Pact
Descender
Blackout
Mutoid Man
Mortals
Polygamyst
The End Men
Lighteater
Beast Modulus
Black Black Black
Jack Burton vs. David Lo-Pan
Our friends, families, ladies,
and everyone else who's given
us a push along the way

The music for this release can be downloaded
via the link below:

www.ingramcontent.com/pod-product-compliance
Lightning Source LLC
Chambersburg PA
CBHW032046040426
42449CB00007B/1007